FEEL THE BEAT

ROCK MUSIC

Tricia Hoffman

Gareth Stevens PUBLISHING

Please visit our website, www.garethstevens.com. For a free color catalog of all our high-quality books, call toll free 1-800-542-2595 or fax 1-877-542-2596

Cataloging-in-Publication Data

Names: Hoffman, Tricia.
Title: Rock music / Tricia Hoffman.
Description: Buffalo, NY : Gareth Stevens Publishing, 2027. | Series: Feel the beat | Includes glossary and index.
Identifiers: ISBN 9781482480696 (pbk.) | ISBN 9781482480702 (library bound) | ISBN 9781482480719 (ebook)
Subjects: LCSH: Rock music--History and criticism--Juvenile literature.
Classification: LCC ML3534.H644 2027 | DDC 781.66--dc23

First Edition

Published in 2027 by
Gareth Stevens Publishing
2544 Clinton Street
Buffalo, NY 14224

Designer: Kathy Walsh/Beeline Media & Design, Inc.
Editor: Tricia Hoffman

Photo credits: Cover, carlos castilla/Shutterstock.com; cover, pp. 1–24 (music note background) Gaianami Design/Shutterstock.com; p 4 Tsuguliev/Shutterstock.com; p 5 @Wiki/Wiki; p 6 & 7 Dan Kosmayer/Shutterstock.com; p 8 Arthur D'Amario III/Shutterstock.com; p 9 Lana Sham, spatuletail/Shutterstock.com; p 10 yakub88/Shutterstock.com; p 11 Daniel DeSlover/Shutterstock.com; p 11 A.PAES/Shutterstock.com; p 12 katatonia82/Shutterstock.com; p 13 Jdrw25/Shutterstock.com; p 14 Bill Raymond/Shutterstock.com; p 16 Master 1305/Shutterstock.com; p 19 Bruce Alan Bennett/Shutterstock.com; p 21 Silivio Tanaka @Wiki/Wiki; p 21 ChrisJamesRyanPhotography/Shutterstock.com; p 22 Cris Fraga/Shutterstock.com; p 23 Photography Stock Ruiz/Shutterstock.com; p 24 Zamrznuti tonovi/Shutterstock.com; p 25 Ben Houdijk/Shutterstock.com; p 26 Zamrznuti Tonovi/Shutterstock.com; p 27 Paul McKinnon, sripfoto, Arthur D'Amario III/Shutterstock.com; p 28 @Wiki/Wiki; p 29 DFree, IgorGolovniov, MLM IMAGES Los Angeles, L Paul Mann/Shutterstock.com

Printed in China

CPSIA compliance information: Batch #QS27GS: For further information contact Gareth Stevens, New York, New York at 1-800-542-2595.

Table of Contents

Get Ready to Rock!

Rock music is one of the most popular kinds of music in the world. People of all ages love it. It makes you feel full of energy. It can be fast or slow. It can be loud or soft. But it always has that special rock sound.

Before rock, most popular music was for adults. But rock is different. It's loud. It's exciting. And sometimes, it's a little wild. It is music that belongs to young people.

Get ready to rock through the world of rock and roll!

Alan Freed

ROCK AND ROLL

The phrase "rock and roll" was originally slang for dancing. A radio DJ named Alan Freed started using it to describe the music in the 1950s, and the name stuck!

The Birth of Rock Music

Rock music was born in America in the 1950s. For years, Black musicians had been playing **blues** and R&B music. Country music was popular with many white Americans. When these music **genres** combined, they created rock and roll!

Many people call Elvis Presley "The King of Rock and Roll." Elvis changed everything. He grew up listening to gospel music in church, blues music from Black musicians, and country music on the radio. When Elvis started performing in 1954, he mixed all these sounds together.

Elvis sang, danced, and played guitar in a new way. No one had seen or heard anything like it!

TOO WILD FOR TV

Television shows would only film Elvis from the waist up. His dancing was too wild for TV! But young people loved him. They had never seen anyone perform with so much energy.

Rock Music Throughout the Years

In the 1960s, British bands became huge stars. The Beatles wrote catchy songs that everyone loved to sing. The Rolling Stones played hard, rough rock music.

The 1970s gave us hard rock and heavy metal. Bands like Led Zeppelin and Black Sabbath played loud and heavy. They used powerful **amplifiers**. Their guitars sounded rough and aggressive.

Punk rock also started in the 1970s. Bands like The Ramones played fast, simple songs that were raw and wild.

The Ramones

BRAND NEW SOUNDS

In the 1960s, Jimi Hendrix played electric guitar in ways no one had heard before. He could make his guitar sound like it was crying or screaming.

In the 1980s, some bands used **synthesizers** and keyboards. MTV started showing music videos on TV. How band members looked became almost as important as how they sounded! Bands like Bon Jovi and Guns N' Roses filled huge stadiums with fans. Hair metal bands wore flashy clothes and had big, teased hair.

Grunge bands were popular in the 1990s. They played raw, emotional rock. Bands like Nirvana, Pearl Jam, and Soundgarden were very different from the flashy 1980s style. These rockers wore regular clothes like flannel shirts and ripped jeans.

Bon Jovi

Guns N' Roses

Soundgarden

In the 2000s, bands like The White Stripes played garage rock with just a guitar and drums. They showed you didn't need a big band to rock hard! Linkin Park mixed rock with hip hop and electronic sounds.

Today, Imagine Dragons mixes rock with electronic dance beats. Twenty One Pilots blends rock, rap, and pop. Greta Van Fleet plays classic rock-style music like bands from the 1970s. Rock music never stops growing!

Linkin Park

Imagine Dragons

What Makes Music "Rock"?

The electric guitar is the heart of most rock songs. Guitarists can make their instruments sound smooth and clean. They can make them sound loud and rough. Some of the most famous rock songs are remembered because of their great guitar **riffs**.

Electric guitar solos let players show off their skills. A guitar solo is when one guitarist takes center stage. They play amazing notes while the rest of the band plays in the background. Guitar solos can be fast and exciting. They can also be slow and beautiful.

Metallica

Drummers keep the beat strong and steady. They typically use a drum kit that includes several drums and cymbals. The bass drum makes a deep boom. The snare drum gives a sharp crack. The cymbals crash and sizzle.

The bass guitar provides the low, rumbling sounds that you can feel in your chest. It works with the drums to create the **rhythm** section. This holds the whole song together. Without it, rock music would sound thin and weak.

Rock singing is not just about sounding pretty. It is about feeling and energy. Singers might sing smooth ballads. They might shout and scream. Some rock singers have high, powerful voices. Others have raspy, rough voices.

Rock music usually has a strong beat. The songs often follow a pattern: verse, **chorus**, verse, chorus. Rock **lyrics** can be about love, problems, fun, or important issues.

What really makes rock music special is the attitude. Rock music has energy and power. It can be wild. It can be thoughtful and deep. But it always has a spirit that makes you want to turn up the volume!

Led Zeppelin

Rock Music Around the World

Rock music started in America, but it quickly spread around the world. Every country added its own special flavor.

In England, rock music became huge in the 1960s. Bands like Queen and The Who became legends. British rock often sounds a bit different from American rock. It mixes in sounds from electronic music and indie styles.

Japan loves rock music too. Japanese rock is called "J-rock." It has its own special style. Some Japanese rock bands like X Japan, The Gazette, and Dir En Grey dress in colorful, wild costumes. Visual Kei is a Japanese rock style where how you look is just as important as the music.

Pete Townshend

A SMASH HIT

Pete Townshend from The Who was famous for smashing his guitars on stage. He broke his first guitar by accident when it hit the ceiling. But the audience loved it so much, he kept doing it!

Dir En Grey

In Latin America, rock music mixes with traditional Latin sounds. Mexican rock bands might blend rock with mariachi music. Brazilian rockers sometimes add samba rhythms.

Australia has produced many famous rock bands like AC/DC that are known for their high-energy hard rock. German bands mix electronic sounds with rock. South African rock sometimes includes traditional African instruments and rhythms. Artists play these instruments alongside electric guitars and drums.

No matter where it's played, rock music brings people together. Fans around the world connect through their love of rock.

Rock Music Today and Tomorrow

Rock music is still alive and rocking! Today's rock bands use computers and technology along with traditional instruments. They can record music in home studios and share it with fans over the internet. Social media helps new rock bands find listeners all over the world.

Rock festivals bring together thousands of fans. Rock bands play at huge events like Coachella and Lollapalooza. People love seeing their favorite bands play live and singing along with other fans.

Bruce Springsteen

MARATHON ROCK CONCERTS

The longest concert ever lasted 453 hours! That's almost 19 days of non-stop music. Different bands took turns playing in Germany in 2016. Rocker Bruce Springsteen is famous for very long concerts too. His shows often last more than three hours.

What will rock music sound like in the future? It will probably keep changing. Maybe future rock bands will use instruments that haven't been invented yet. Or maybe rock music will travel to outer space as humans explore other planets.

As long as people want music that's powerful, exciting, and makes them feel alive, rock music will never die. The spirit of rock and roll will live on forever.

So, turn up the volume. Feel that beat. Let's rock!

Chris Hadfield

David Bowie

ROCKING IN SPACE

Astronauts have played rock music in space! Commander Chris Hadfield recorded a music video on the International Space Station. He sang David Bowie's "Space Oddity" while floating!

Rock Music Superstars

Get ready to rock! Rock and roll music has been exciting fans for more than 70 years. These amazing superstars changed music forever with their powerful voices, incredible guitar skills, and unforgettable performances. Let's meet some of the greatest rock stars in history!

Chuck Berry
1950s-2010s

Chuck Berry wrote and sang some of the first rock and roll songs. Many people say he invented rock and roll music! Chuck Berry could play guitar amazingly fast and made it look easy. He wrote songs that told stories about teenagers, cars, and having fun.

Janis Joplin
1960s-1970s

Janis Joplin had a powerful, raspy voice. She could make people cry with her singing because she put so much feeling into every word. She was one of the first women to become a huge rock star. She showed girls they could be rock stars too.

Freddie Mercury
1970s-1990s

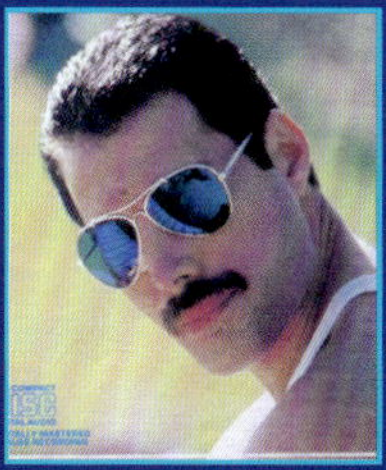

Freddie Mercury was the singer for the band Queen. Freddie could sing in four different octaves, which means he could sing super high and super low notes. He sang "We Will Rock You" and "We Are the Champions," which are still played at sports games everywhere!

Billie Joe Armstrong
1990s-today

Billie Joe Armstrong is the singer and guitarist for the punk rock band Green Day. He started playing music and wrote his first song when he was only five years old! Green Day has won five Grammy Awards and sold more than 75 million records.

Hayley Williams
2000s-today

Hayley Williams is the singer for the band Paramore. She started her band when she was only 13 years old. Her band plays energetic rock music about real feelings and problems. She encourages young people to be confident and express themselves.

Yungblud
2010s-today

Yungblud mixes punk rock with modern sounds. He has lots of energy and jumps around on stage. He wears make-up and encourages kids to be themselves and celebrate being unique. His music is loud and talks about being different and standing up for what's right.

Glossary

amplifiers (AM-pluh-fye-urz): devices that make sound louder

blues (blooz): sad, soulful music that helped create rock

chorus (KOR-uhs): the part of a song that is repeated after each verse

genres (ZHAHN-ruhz): types or kinds of music, like hip hop, rock, or pop

lyrics (LIR-iks): the words of a song that tell the story

rhythm (RITH-uhm): the repeated pattern of sound or movement in music, poetry, or dance

riffs (rifs): repeated musical patterns; a catchy melody that the guitar plays over and over

synthesizers (SIN-thuh-sye-zurz): electronic instruments that can create many different sounds using computers and technology

Fact Check

1. When was rock music born?

a. 1930s b. 1950s c. 1970s

2. What is a guitar solo?

a. When a guitarist plays guitar alone at home.

b. When one guitarist takes center stage and plays fancy notes.

c. When a guitar costs a lot of money.

3. Which rock star was famous for smashing guitars on stage?

a. Elvis Presley b. Pete Townshend c. Chuck Berry

Answers: 1. b, 2. b, 3. b

On the Internet

22 Best Rock Songs for Kids to Listen

www.thebridalbox.com/articles/best-rock-songs-for-kids-listen/

Check out these rock songs! How many have you heard before?

Rock Music Facts for Kids

https://kids.kiddle.co/Rock_music

Explore the history of rock music and see photos of rock stars from the past and present.

Publisher's note to educators and parents: Our editors have carefully reviewed these websites to ensure that they are suitable for students. Many websites change frequently, however, and we cannot guarantee that a site's future contents will continue to meet our high standards of quality and educational value. Be advised that students should be closely supervised whenever they access the internet.

Index

About the Author

Tricia Hoffman is a writer, editor, reader, and runner. She lives in Columbus, Ohio, with her husband and two sons. Her favorite kind of rock is alternative rock from the 1990s, especially bands like Third Eye Blind, Matchbox Twenty, and Eve 6. She enjoys music of all kinds and loves to sing along.